In cricket you need to score runs and protect the

bails

wicket

stumps

The batters have to hit the ball to stop it hitting the wicket.

bowler
/**boal**er/

The bowlers attempt to knock the bails off the wicket and get all of the batters out.

Here is a cricket ground.

pitch

The wickets are at
the ends of the pitch.

Runs are scored when the batters run between the wickets.

willow
/**wi**lσa/

The best cricket bats are carved from willow wood.

It is very hard and
will not splinter or dent.

Cricket balls are solid and very hard.

wicket keeper

Batters and wicket keepers have thick pads and helmets to keep the ball from hitting them.

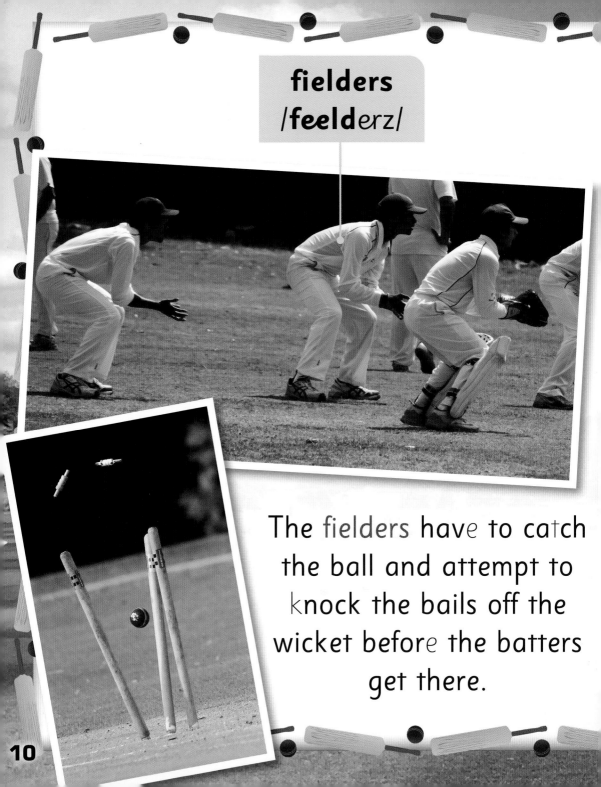

fielders
/**feeld**erz/

The fielders have to catch the ball and attempt to knock the bails off the wicket before the batters get there.

If they catch the
ball, the batter is out.

If a batter is out before they have scored a run, they are said to be "out for a duck"!

quack